Usborne
Sticker Dolly Dressing
Trick or treat

Written by
Fiona Watt

Designed & illustrated by
Non Figg

Contents

Pumpkin patch

It's the week before Halloween and Aimee, Jude, and Ellie are visiting a farm where you can pick your own pumpkins. Aimee can't wait to carve a creepy face on the one that she's chosen.

Aimee

Jude

Ellie

Spooky house

The dolls are decorating Casey's house, hoping to encourage trick-or-treaters to knock on the door. They've added a scary cat silhouette, pumpkin lanterns… and lots and lots of spiders!

Alesha

Ryan

Casey

Creepy crafts

The dolls are preparing to go trick-or-treating. Zahra's decorating an old T-shirt with a pumpkin face, Jake is designing a skeleton costume and Billie is finishing a snake made from an old scarf that she'll wrap around her shoulders.

Zahra

Billie

Jake

7

Witch dance

Lexie, Cody, and Lola have been asked to perform a party trick before they are given any treats, so they're doing their special witchy dance. They've spent ages in the days before Halloween perfecting it and making sure that they all move together.

Lexie

Cody

Lola

Finding costumes

At the last minute, Mila, Tara, and Paige have decided to go trick-or-treating. They're hunting for things in Tara's bedroom that they could wear.

Mila

Tara

Paige

Carving pumpkins

The dolls have carefully cut the tops off their pumpkins and are scooping out the seeds and pulp. Marissa is going to carve a face with a toothy grin, while Kieran is planning to turn his pumpkin into a cat.

Kieran

Callie

Marissa

Face painting

Alina is putting the finishing touches on Ethan's face paint. He's impressed at how spooky he looks! Lauren is brushing her cheeks with bright red powder to complete her clown face.

Alina

Ethan

Lauren

Treats

Jack and Malia knocked on Bonnie's door. She doesn't want to have any tricks played on her, so she brings out a bowl of treats right away.

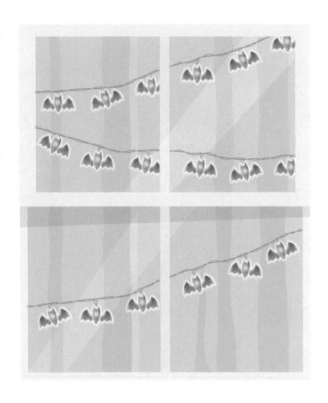

Bonnie

Jack

Malia

Animal antics

The dolls are going from house to house. When they knock on the doors, Megan roars like a monster, Piper bounces like a bunny, and Jay flaps his arms while squawking like a bird. They hope that their friends will be impressed!

Megan

Piper

Jay

Grab a bag

Freya is trying to feel brave as she plunges
her hand into a tub to grab something.
Will she be lucky and pull out a treat, or will
it be a Halloween trick? What do you think?

Freya

Jade

Ashley

Scary scarecrows

Ben knocked on the door then scurried away, while Lara and Carly hid behind a hedge. As the front door opened, the dolls, dressed in scruffy scarecrow costumes, jumped up and shook their hands in the air.

Lara

Carly

Ben

Costume selfie

Before they get ready for bed, Sam, Kyle, and Asha pose for a photo in their Halloween costumes. They'll send it to each other as a memory of the fun evening they've spent together.

Sam

Kyle

Asha

Additional illustration by Stella Baggott

First published in 2023 by Usborne Publishing Limited, 83-85 Saffron Hill, London EC1N 8RT, United Kingdom. usborne.com

Pumpkin patch

Aimee's pumpkin

Aimee's outfit

Jude's pumpkin

Jude's scarf, hat and sneakers

Jude's outfit

Ellie's outfit

Spooky house

Pages 4-5

Alesha's skirt and top

Alesha's boots

Casey's clothes

Ryan's outfit

Jake's shirt

Billie's dress

Creepy crafts

Pages 6-7

Zahra's outfit

Billie's boots

Lexie's hat

Put Lexie's skirt on before her cape.

Cody's hat

Cody's costume

Lola's boots

Put Lola's top on before her skirt.

Finding costumes

Tara's sneakers

Mila's outfit

Mila's headscarf

Tara's clothes

Paige's clothes

Put Tara's top on after her bottoms.

Tara's hat

Kieran's outfit

Callie's hat

Callie's boots

Callie's outfit

Marissa's hat

Marissa's outfit

Face painting

Pages 14-15

Alina's boots

Face paint for Alina to hold

Ethan's face and outfit

Alina's clothes

Alina's headscarf

Ethan's hat, but he's not wearing it.

Lauren's painted face

Lauren's costume

Treats

Bonnie's headband

Jack's outfit

Jack's treat bucket

Bonnie's clothes

A bowl for Bonnie to hold

Jack's costume

Malia's boots

Malia's clothes and bag

Megan's boots

Piper's boots

Megan's monster costume

Piper's costume

Jay's clothes

Grab a bag

Pages 20-21

Freya's outfit

Put Ashley's bottoms on before his top.

Freya's bag

Ashley's mask

Ashley's jacket and shoes

Jade's outfit

Ashley's bag

Put the barrel below Freya's hand.

Scary scarecrows

Pages 22-23

Carly's shirt

Lara's hat and top

Carly's hat

Carly's bowtie

Ben's hat and jacket

Costume selfie

Page 24

Sam's top

Kyle's hood

Asha's robot mask

Sam's bandana and hook

A robot control panel